PRAISE FOR A

MW00364496

"*In Anatomy of Want*, hunting mus~~l~~ ~~themselves~~ ~~drink that~~
themselves into poetry through the imagination of Daniel Lee. This is a
remarkable first book, a set of hymns, a set of prayers in installments from
the young poet's mouth to the ears of the reader, the precariously beloved, an
eavesdropping divinity."　　　　　—Scott Hightower, *Part of the Bargain*

"Daniel's poems mesmerize and engage in revelatory ways. Sexy and
profound, this significant debut is a heartfelt contribution to contemporary
poetry. An essential new voice worth celebrating."
　　　　　　　　　　　　　　　—Emanuel Xavier, *Pier Queen*

"Daniel Lee's work wrestles with desire, melancholy, family and belonging.
His work celebrates the beauty and limits of language with blood-stirring
sensuality and lyricism. His use of non-Western classical forms shows the
universality of the human need for poetry and makes a dazzling juxtaposition
with his evocative use of English."
　　　　　　　　　—Annapurna Potluri Schreiber, *The Grammarian*

"Daniel Lee's new book of poetry, *Anatomy of Want* employs a masterful
command of language that weaves allusions to his Chinese family, love, sex &
the body. Scaling the nature of desire and longing, Lee's poems offer moments
of reversal and emotional intricacy that are by turns playful, intellectually
engaging, formally challenging and deeply pleasurable. His articulation of
emptiness made me sad about life but excited and hopeful, too. A remarkable
debut."　　　　　　　　　　　　　　—Tomas Mournian, *hidden*

"Daniel Lee's debut collection is a much needed breath of fresh air on the
brow of a world going mad with fever. His verse are songs of testimony,
history, and bittersweet storytelling. I am proud to see his poems brought
together in these beautiful pages. All hail Daniel, the new prince of lyricism!
Rise here and rest in his words!"　　　　—Shane Allison, *Slut Machine*

ANATOMY OF WANT

Daniel W. K. Lee

QUEER MOJO
A Rebel Satori Imprint
New Orleans

Published in the United States of America by
REBEL SATORI PRESS
www.rebelsatori.com

Library of Congress Control Number:2019953426

Dedicated to the memory of Wayne Buidens

ACKNOWLEDGEMENTS

I thank my inspirations (could-have-been) beloveds; as well as Mae Karas for being such an excellent reader and critic; Scott Hightower for being my mentor at Gallatin and teaching me so much; Gabriel Cohen for his hopefulness, my parents for their sacrifices, Tomas Mournian and Shane Allison for their unshakable belief in me, and of course Manoella González for reinventing the sum of one plus one.

I also want to thank my readers and creative conspirators over the years besides those mentioned above—Daniel Just, Annapurna Potluri Schreiber, Shane Lukas—for their critiques, praise, and support. Sven Davisson for taking a chance on me and my poetry. To my family—chosen and blood—including my sweet dog Camden with whom I could not thrive without. Thank you all for your confidence and love, for making me laugh, keeping me sane, and often, just staying out of my way. I am indebted.

Finally, grateful acknowledgment is made to the editors of the following publications where these poems—some in slightly different form—first appeared:

"Remedies" was previously published in *Fourteen Hills: The SFSU Review*, vol. 9, no. 1

"Kama's Clay" published in *Lodestar Quarterly*, issue 1, www.lodestarquarterly.com

"La Cocina" was previously published in *Narcolepsy Arms*, issue 1, www.narcolepsyarms.com

Part I of "At Risk", "Cuddling" was previously published in *The Gay & Lesbian Review*, vol. 11, no. 2, March-April 2004

"Anatomy of Want" was previously published in *modern words*, no. 8

"The Rain" was previously published in *Poetic Voices Without*

Borders (Gival Press, 2005)

"Compliments to the Cook" and "Nipping" was previously published in *Chiron Review*, vol. 81, Winter 2005

"Home" and "The Night" was previously published in *LYNX*, October 2008, www.ahapoetry.com/ahalynx/

"Secrets" was previously published in *Poetic Voices Without Borders 2* (Gival Press, 2009)

"Ties" was previously published in *Eating Her Wedding Dress: A Collection of Clothing Poems* (Ragged Sky Press, 2009)

"Rooftop" and "Brazilian Jiujitsu" was previously published in *Mythium*, no. 3

"no" was previously published in *Weave*, issue 6

"In the Dark" was previously published in *Agenda.*, vol. 47, no.1

"First Aid" was previously published in *Off the Rocks*

"In Your Arms" was previously published in *Psychic Meatloaf*, issue 5.

"Bastard" was previously published in *BLOOM*, vol. 4, no. 1, Spring 2012

"Death of *Saudade*" was previously published in *Diverse Voices Quarterly*, vol. 3, issues 9 & 10

"Accounts of Lucifer" published in *Conclave: A Journal of Character*, issue 3, Spring 2012

"The Way We Wore Young" published in *Oxford Poetry*, XIV.2, Winter 2012

"Gospel of Mark" published in *Dialogist*, vol. 1, issue 2, www.dialogist.org

"Biography of a Heretic" and "proximity" published in *The Boiler*, no. 8, Summer 2013, www.theboilerjournal.com

"Apocryphal" published in *The Cape Rock*, vol. 40, no. 1, Spring 2013

"Making Dinner" published in *and/or*, vol. 2, Spring 2014

"Commitment" published in *White Stag*, vol. 1, issue 2

"Beginnings" published in *Berkeley Poetry Review*, no. 43, Spring 2016

Contents

ANATOMY OF WANT

NO

became a reckoning
a door ajar
a letter, which read:

> *Dear Manoella,*
>
> *My eyes are in orbit. It is July 4th and Boston's 10pm sky is cross-stitched with gunpowder and technicolor. Blue comets dazzle through.*

became:

> *She is worried that I might give in to you. By "you" she means, "malignant longings that don't stay single file along the ribs that wear your face like an act of nature."*

became hearsay
a big, grape Kool-Aid smile
crows feet and near-sightedness

became ravenous
a red violin concerto
strands of pubic hair in an envelope
an affair with a sharp object
echoes of JM:

"Somehow the thought, put in those words, hurt less"

or Ephraim:

"I go behind the falls./Make him be there, my angel, and alive—/Anything you say I will believe."

became passing through moods like neighborhoods
an apple thief
hiccups of rain

became like a suicide
prayer—in installments:

Je vous salue, Marie, pleine de grace...

became the last syllables of summer

Sainte Marie, Mère de Dieu, Priez pour nous, pauvres pécheurs

became defrocked
not having been
washed by words

SECRETS
[to C.L.]

Black currants and bergamot infuse the deep secrets.
The bar serves fevered water as sangria to steep secrets.

Your phone's in love, you say. It calls you without me.
Has it drunk-dialed and left after the beep secrets?

A light bulb is loosened behind the wrought iron gate;
a square under the stairs where we'd heap secrets?

Scanning the dedications in his rare editions,
the ones missing my name belong with the cheap secrets.

Winter's kimono sleeves whirl, wetting the eyes;
a clever cover in daylight while we seep secrets.

An accomplice of rapture rewinds to the crime:
"The shoebox falls twice...between breaths creep secrets."

He peels back his hood and with it hesitation.
Let want be canine. I'll put to sleep secrets.

For food, for thrill, for fucking, the appetite asks:
Isn't a hunger left hungry free to reap secrets?

Your mouth, Daniel's: they've turned into honeycomb.
Hint: their sweet walls—once?—did more than keep secrets.

3

COMPLIMENTS TO THE COOK

Somewhere,
you are gilding onions
with grease and *achiote* paste,
and on the sizzling bottom
of the frying pan
a sun is reborn.
Your hands, splashed
with port wine birthmarks,
rub meat with sea salt,
cumin powder, cracked
peppercorns, causing
temperatures as distant as
Tapachula to crest like waves
of heat from your open oven.
Naughty thing, was this
your ploy to get those hungry
jimadores along roadside *agave*
fields to shuck their shirts,
baring lean bellies to busloads
of American retirees en route
to Lake Chapala; and over there,
near the iguana farm, you
inadvertently wilted the embroidered
flowers on Tía Gloria's dress.
Limonada, horchata, agua—
your clear breath cools like.

4

And oh that slim, strutting
hymn you sent, like so much steam
I might also have missed,
had I uncovered my eyes.

BASTARD

[for Aaron Bonventre]

Ten yrs old   eyes shiny like crude oil
used to wonder who
supplied these endless eyes

But clearly   was you
rotten vision not inherited   instead
conditioned
            weekends locked in
            basement   bedroom
reading   (no other choice)
Treasure Island   *The Hardy Boys*   *Nancy Drew*
over over   over past
stung ray'd eyes   past
saltwater (mourning tears
for Mom's
            buried eyes)
past uglypity   palerage
for letting new bride   (merciless beauty)
win
prizing those eyes that
should have been   watching me
then the youngest

            instead

a career

in solitude
started   so by fifteen
when sent away
        "emancipated" (the law calls it)
by stepmom's plot of perjury   ("attempted murder")
        that Port Authority desertion
        only
embellished could-have-but-never-gaves:
eyeglasses   driving lessons   birthday candles

32   still a bastard   that boy still spills into this face
that why you passed
not recognizing   eyes you made?
I've traded books for   dvd marathons
aisle seats in movie theatres
        w/out company
not having to speak/care
        un-anguished
but now   here
asked you to talk   yet
I've been littering
parts of speech   like
cigarette butts   because
how   why
interrogate about
        abandonedthingspast   (this time, meaning you)

I remind you my bland name   again

but meant to say:

"Dad" (a formality)
can you bear to see
how

      ruthlessly
      and unfinished

I do
pardon
you?

BIOGRAPHY OF A HERETIC

I memorized the chapter with you
at age five, soup ladles for hands,
digging to Fujian for the starving ones
your mother swore would eat liver
without being asked twice,
because they knew obedience
made boys men.

You never met those sons
who grew up to be everything
you aren't, did you?

I hear they have them in Spain now:
Moorish bachelors built like fortresses,
whose eyes are crusades
converting infidels like you—

who loved God more than me.

IN THE DARK

Not just mine, but your intentions stain in the dark.
Re-christened "temptation," gathers like rain in the dark.

By what regime of lotion, genes, or god,
are such soft slopes justified in being vain in the dark?

Smash the dinner plates for this extinguished distance!
I'll pour the shots, darling, to drain in the dark.

The clothes measure a man? Says who: when patterns
from paisleys to pinstripes are all plain in the dark.

O blameless boy, of the bare way we failed you:
you were, with no wind, a weathervane in the dark.

Where ever God's hiding the cure for your death sentence,
for you I'm overturning every grain in the dark.

When all else is hijacked, I'll leave you the hymn.
The ear never loses the refrain in the dark.

Is the dark pitiless to prolong the punishment?
Reliving your whisper is worth the pain in the dark.

Before caving in to lips pursed into an apology,
give me a chance to at least complain in the dark.

Silence—be warned—is a consummate politician:
an ally in light, bane in the dark.

A toast to ignorance for prolonging bliss!
Why sober a thrill if we remain in the dark?

I fall into fantasy. How do I know? You are saying,
"This word 'yours', Daniel, could you explain...in the dark?"

ACCOUNTS OF LUCIFER

I.

I obeyed Him; kowtow to Adam I would not do.
I, the true monotheist, do not envy the living.
This Fall must continue: to
perfect a God who could forget giving

that earlier command: Bow to no other
but me. Thus, Hell's my right to bear.
The burning lake is easy to smother
but could I suffer more gloriously elsewhere?

Dear Lord, my God, I'm rising beneath Your foot.
There will be martyrs on both sides: cured
of immortality and castes of grace. I believe

in what You withhold: fairness. Forgiveness cannot
expire, but does. With miracles scarce, un-shared,
could You survive with so little love?

II.

"Christ, you are God's most novel invention.
Before He appended Himself into a careless
trinity, it was I who held His exalted attention.
Though without His favor, I am still fearless.

So what is the point of Man's salvation?
He has been cruel to more than mothers
not his own. Pain follows like a migration
after the "righteous" slaughter of brothers.

Be sure to know, war is not what I've wanted—
it is a spectacle. I prefer sane, not demented,
revolt. Nothing is more tasteless than murder.

I confounded my Adversary when I stole
His minions of light. I shall restore the Order.
I, the first given free will of those without a soul."

III.

From Gabriel's arrogant eyes I took flight
forbidding him to hear the sigh that fell
from the throat round with regret. Right
here, only in Hell does my face cover well

every trace of loss. I envied Mary; her
sorrow like a wolf howling over lands
immodestly. No lament gnarled in her
belly. No grief like glass ground in her hands.

Behold, I'm not wretched! Let the seraphs despise
me if it doubles my dark radiance! When
I survive the end of time, meekness

will revisit the Messiah. His shaded eyes
will dart. The Savior's flagrant weakness
is his humanity and equals the hope of men.

IV.

Does language suffice to state how Your face stuns
with its impossible beauty? It's almost oppression
knotting syllables from those desert tongues
to represent us. I wish to never lose this position:

Beloved. Lucifer, this name I wear
because You composed it so, falls over You in oceans
of devotion. Water unfolds everywhere,
and I am barefoot in a sky without seasons.

I prostrate solely for You, my Love. Choice
is not a consideration. You are every one of them.
No matter what, You are every one of them.

Who could refuse You when You use that petulant voice?
If I were Your sweet slanderer, I'd tell them,
I conquered God with my love! Rejoice! Rejoice!

V.

How could we the Jinn be subordinate to him—
Adam—the caliph of clay, few of wives,
whose only power given by Him
was to name Earth's minor lives?

How easy for Iblis, on that destined day,
haiif whispered into Hawwa's head,
to pervert the pair. With the fruit they
were forbidden to savor, she fed

her husband knowledge; Thus ashamed to tell
all-knowing Allah, they came to know labor:
of birth, of field, outside Eden as a neighbor.

Now we the soldiers of smokeless fire center
our ire against humanity! Jahannam's citadel
smolders. Al-Shaitan's Man's mandated tormentor!

VI.

"Lucifer" I prefer, as in Morning Star, a stud in sky
hurled down diamond-like, stoning the yet real
(the mastery of Man), O Adam. Reveal

your grade of purity, as I, God's Prosecutor, don't decry
your sins, only gild them like medallions. Believe: I exist
for you—to test your piety in the divine court. Surprised?
Even the stained serve Him. Weaknesses memorized,
the epilogues ordained, are your sons fit to resist?

Indeed they'll excel in Law: an eye for an eye,
a fist to a face, or a gun in its place.
Easier to get even than bury shame; your race

will hedge damnation like an eloquent lie.
The heart—with no other choice—obeys
the Light. Beware the stars. It is time to die.

DAY OF THE DEAD

Plow the sky with the sun
in the year of rust.
Done.

Foot resents wing
That miraculous limb—
Of sorts.

On paper,
An epic clothesline
Hung.

Stuck on the cheese
Your vanity
Saves face?

It is your right,
Your sweet scowl,
your wasted night.

Like leaves,
Souvenirs of decay
Brought home.

Damned, or humored
The ancient
Don't stop.

Who's counting
The moth holes
In every façade?

A thousand or so
quidam
Part.

Supplicant, am I?
Anonymous groins
Dignified.

Palms face each other
Not in prayer—
In reflex.

My nevertheless woman.
Secular stigmata.
Cathedral of your cunt.

Coming
Last.
Fast

Crescendo.
Refrain
Of notes like caviar on water cracker.

Again
Like science
For the gold medal.

Why hide
The Golden Horde?
Hushed hooves?

Why the Hun
("Scourge of God"),
Not Biblical?

Electrical
Miracle—
Typical.

Felony metonym
metaphor
For bread

O silver Enemy,
Tarnish
Tarnished.

Shriek
When it smokes.
Or we'll forget who burns.

IN YOUR ARMS

This holocaust of clocks (their movement entombed in your arms)
left behind borrowed time quietly consumed in your arms.

Half-true: I have no sense, *querido*. I struggle for you.
Whatever ever made sense limps, doomed in your arms.

The stink of longing inside the misanthrope's throat
like a shitpile it just mushroomed in your arms.

Beatify? Why? Because Lilies of the Nile
in the desert of winter bloomed in your arms?

An avatar, you are, by the way you've tamed hurricanes
and strands of lightning groomed in your arms.

Fall over her first in a hesitant drizzle.
She's seen how a monsoon loomed in your arms.

A shortage of reasons to see me, and demand high,
an economy of ruses instantly boomed in your arms.

To compose—prematurely?—a requiem for us,
the practice of letting go resumed in your arms.

For lawless knowledge of the edges of your tongue:
guilt and innocence presumed in your arms.

Rumi's unread revolution: "Love cannot be said."
In other words, silence is assumed in your arms.

The chin scar is the index concealed on Daniel's face.
Where was the last hand to reach it exhumed? In your arms.

FIRST AID

[for C.L.]

If I slash my ring-fingertip w/an X-acto knife:
against OSHA regulations, you should tenderly
risk your lips, knead the red edges together.

BRAZILIAN JIUJITSU

[for M. Bennett]

After the mats had been glazed
with Clorox like a pastry, the delayed giggle
escaped my throat long after you'd said,
"It's only gay if you look into each other's
eyes." We had been training for several months,
building my vocabulary of chokes, holds, passes,
crushes—each one a more nuanced entanglement
of sweat, limbs, and defiance. Demos
necessitating bare torsos to be pasted together
like a Martha Stewart craft project maintained
an air of instruction, if not the musk of something more.
A nifty surprise this body has been—no?—with its
limber and sleuthy strength. A yoga-supple shoulder,
nimble *capoeira* legs enlist those extra steps required
to hear the taps that signify a submission.
The first time I had put you in "The Electric Chair"
or "The Rack" was kinda bad-ass, you'd have to admit—
I, being such novice. If you hadn't noticed though,
rumbling is perfect for control queens,
(Yeah, I'm calling you a queen),
but not because it is some test of will,
triumph over another; instead, the way we atone:
finding the fun in being at each other's mercy.

ANYMORE

Who taught you to undo those not near anymore
like cries of wolf you don't hear anymore?

You sun his jealousy into a canopy of vines.
Are you part of a sky that won't appear anymore?

Coffins without bodies get buried with hope—
my arms cannot bear who disappear anymore.

The blood of the Unheld births the lament of the blues,
and does it rise to the eyes just as clear anymore?

I can't help but be suspect. My tears fib too.
Sincerity's so cinch, words aren't dear anymore.

"Don't waste your limerence," plundered ribs sing,
"Just a vacancy, love don't live here anymore."

But at what temperature was Daniel emptied?
Frozen, he fell. No one to fear. Anymore.

SURRENDER

Its ways all counted, measured Love tries surrender:
(stripped of infinity) bears the flag that cries surrender.

Swiftly, antique angel, creep down to witness;
eternity expires. I'm ready to reprise surrender.

The Graeae say: "We are more god-like than Perseus can claim—
having swallowed years without sunrise, surrender."

I'll chase you in all manner: from madwoman to martyr.
But who will I be if you come with surprise surrender?

Bring matches, switchblades and lend them to me
to terrorize those heartbeats that summarize surrender.

Daniel, "Your face is what religion tries to remember"
You're your own heretic in that callous disguise: surrender.

ROOFTOP

Are we ironic in this cityscape
of luxury and capitalist peaks
that, when needy, could simply
lean across Manhattan to rest
beneath each other's chins?

The sun's surplus hauls itself
through tree tops, kitchenette
windows, some photographer's
camera lens. Tourists will declare
the weather's beauty and get sunburned,
as will seasoned construction workers
lunching on deli sandwiches and bravado
amongst the scaffolding.

Stories above Broadway, I am squinting
and alone with a Tupperware of curried
leftovers, the turmeric staining my nails.
Between these eyelashes, progress appears vertical.

Is up thus the direction of moving-on?

Then it's no use to run away
when even minor loves are
so heavy, so hard, so horizontal.

LA COCINA

Framed by Spanish eyes,
they'll eat pieces of him
like *tapas*
with coarse
mouths and wicked
tongues, planting bites
like kisses.

He'll roast in the heated
purr of R—
> back arched like
> a down-turned parenthesis

> fork fingers cleaved to
> ass, rolling nakedness
> like choice meats on
> cooking spits

> the temperature just shy
> of gourmet.

Across the ocean, he'll
lust like Lorca between
ceviche-white teeth
that'll chew his nipples
like uncured olives

while here
in his house,
bitter.

WITHOUT YOU

O Beloved! Who's to blame for angels who rise without you?
Disloyal God! For this I reveal how to baptize without you!

Where is it then—this alleged logic—if Pleasure has no arithmetic.
Should you find it, I'll still discard that linear disguise without you.

The language of tea in the soothsayer's cup recorded the heart's
        allegory:
Out-classed I am by History's marine—Tomorrow cries—*without*
        you!

There is nowhere (not even the grave) to sneak outside the
        bloodlines.
Loath not the discreet inheritance that hazel'd your eyes without
        you.

Is it true? Joy everyday? Then how are captive tears counted?
The recipe calls for cayenne for the tongue complies without you.

Love instructs: Defeat swift Atalanta with these golden apples.
No one wins—she doesn't yet know—the slightest prize without
        you.

Miserly Owl, the nocturnal accountant, tallies your failures (1!):
You did not budge a mountain, but the big sky sighs without you.

Harbinger! Never was I the same man...and even less, more a fool.
Again let's share a hemisphere—my side's unwise without you.

Do you need a paladin equipped with freckled shoulders too?
You shake your head no. You lie. The mirror decries without you.

The solo for the 10,000 Things starts Silence and ends Echo.
"Then the last note must be yours!" the *erhu* replies. Without you.

I had not mentioned (I thought you knew) eschewing *saudade*
        means
"a memory of musk, the rebel face of hope" dutifully dies without
        you.

Until now, you—alone—sent men away in this Memoir of Panic.
But Daniel's will turn unwritten, if the rest implies: Without you.

VIGNETTES AFTER A BREAKUP

1.
Long before the alarm, mornings require a reckoning.
The gut is smooth and empty – the previous day's resilience
pours out on the mattress. The sunlight makes explicit
such matters leave no stain.

2.
Breakfast is a mine field where one must avoid cinnamon—
the undetonated flavor haunting bowls of oatmeal and yogurt.

3.
There's a membrane at the northbound bus stop that staves off
sobbing. Only no telling what song will pierce it.

4.
As with aluminum cans, collecting distractions is a full-time
occupation. Overtime not mandatory, but best to work to
exhaustion.

5.
A myth that sharks must keep moving lest they suffocate.
They have known all along that sometimes motion
is the sole thing to keep us from crashing.

KAMA'S CLAY

after Richard Howard

For the adored,
mine is its own fanged mutiny, expectant
like age.
Yours, a venerated mandate unacquainted
with its sway.

Mine wakes—the tardy bird.
Yours reclines—maharajah.

As in war,
mine plays the flag-bearer—hapless
contender.
Yours seizes, more like Caesar.

Fashioned so
mine borders a fool—gambling without
the Devil.
Yours, a philosopher—circumspect
practitioner.

That is to say,
mine is a monologue awaiting echoes.
Yours: mouth to mouth.

TIES

I am looking for irony among
these lengths of silk
stitched with Italian surnames,
trademarks of English refinement,
and sentimentalities ready to be loosened
like the half-Windsor knots
I'd abandon for one last turn
at hanging about your neck.

NIPPING

Before
the onslaught
of hydrangea
calla lilies
or other
petals of disclosure
humming the color
of your nipples
or the fragrance
of your last illicit kiss

Shhh...

maybe
your buds
aren't safe
with me.

HOME

Where were you finding me—everywhere not home?
As if a rearview mirror, is your blind spot home?

What is fair in love and war? Only fire? Ashes?
Men who perfected burning always, never got home.

God in shame, even angels refused the Holy Land;
None surrendered Jerusalem. Everyone fought home.

History will not restore him. No, dying was his ticket.
When else—save dying—is diaspora brought home?

A nomad in exile draws his blinds, vanishes to where?
Where nobody else thought. Nobody thought home.

P.S. Daniel, I left to become disaster's first orphan.
On the page I found you, in the poem I sought home.

REMEDIES

[for Daniel Just]

I.

My mothers say
the dim should eat
the heads of steamed fish
to flood ignorant wind
with the wisdom of rivers.
And for limbs and foreheads
fevered from chasing worthwhile
men with accents and books,
they advise a bath of limes
rubbed on without regard
to seeds.

II.

Today I bought a clay pot
and make-shift envelopes
hiding dried sea horses
and *tienchi* blossoms.
Ma, are these the medicines
to brew out the poverty
of a son bloated with skulls?
Would you not say
how smart I am to be kissed

past hunger?

What if he says he tasted limes?

III.

Cut lemon grass stalks
the length of your ease
and add slices
of ginger as thick
as his laughter
into a pan
of boiled rainwater.
Then lean
like eavesdroppers
above the steam
while whispering
in his ear the meanings
of your names:
'just' 'bright' 'cool'
'plum' 'illustrious' 'strong'
to sweat away uncertainty.

ANATOMY OF WANT

Alas, I have found you nowhere near
those torpid cities as far as Kuching
that I crossed like some martyr dragged
down from Paradise. Along the roads

between hamlets built on whispers,
the armless world seemed to applaud
mockingly for all the rummaged
geographies left beneath my heel.

Perhaps you fancied me overturning
the Mediterranean and Pacific,
mining the graves of other men's
ineloquent desires, in search of you

(who made foolishness my vocation
while I wrote missives to unnamed
gods protesting your discretion
to ride the Downtown 9 train

while I silently sobbed on the Uptown).
But alas I have found you
where you always were:
harbored in the strings, those

'no strings attached' strings,
those umbilical strings, that gave life
to poems of mourning, poems of lust,
poems of surrender, of retaliation, of rebellion,

tomorrow's poems, yesterday's,
and even that short provocative one
born days ago for the first poet I ever kissed,
whose red hair and fucking are yet other poems

awaiting paper beds. There behind me, I drew
your ghostly curtains and saw your irises grinning,
transforming into all the eyes I have ever coveted.
But your still obscure anatomy, safely guarded

among those strings like a sultan,
was aware of why I could never
meet men and not insist on strings:
strings make men unordinary. They tow

us along so men may catch us dreaming
of them after dinner; leash us so we
may crawl in and out of their voices;
they leave faith unnecessary

to believe an untimely reply more than suggests
rejection of our affection, and yet ascend
friendship into a worthwhile consolation.
Oh the theatre we freely give you!

You who can afford to be smug in your house
(who need not maps to return there), we are poorly
equipped to sever your home even at our most savage,
even at our most reflective (brandishing mirrored shields

at your best Medusan guise). Yes, I know well
the properties of stone. Your gorgon scalp of strings
made sculptures of men who refused me.
All at once, I wish to massacre you

and your conceited avatars when New York
closes its polluted eyes without a beloved
to watch me carry the moon,
and burn incense for your favor:

so when the great sheets of light
litter the world, he will write to me,
and I him, more threaded poems
doing little to escape you.

UNFIT

There are teeth marks
        all over where you left
my house shivering

        a door chewed like leather
or a familiar despair
        I do not blame you

for assailing me with tears
        as you left
that 1 a.m. phone call

        bleeding another man's
voice still ringing
        your heart

you knew what he was
        is
not a rival nor you one too

        I am sorry you think
I could be your champion
        ease you off a world

without a lover
        or better days
forgive me (if you wish)

        for giving you hope
I did not promise
        or wished to send

you away
        in mourning
when the sun resurrected

        I am no mightier
or wiser
        than wanting

to save you near me
        so mistake for weakness
(if you must)

        I cannot
(with you loving)
        rescue you from you

HOROSCOPE

[for Shane Lukas]

Don't believe that the stars don't see
how your booty demands
that the seat of those Old Navy jeans
hang on all them unlawful curves.

No use pretending you don't understand
how I could get you off like a porno,
why for a Leo, you're much too humble
to not mention that hot, conceited ass.

OF SORROW

Weeping Siddhatta, overcome by a coup of sorrow,
someday you'll awaken to disarm the you of sorrow.

To prevent re-infection, take this precaution:
bleach the rice bowls of any residue of sorrow.

Ancient medication: drink past contemplation.
Be numbed into amber by a daily brew of sorrow.

Get used to it angels! You will not soothe forever.
Not even God can revise what is true of Sorrow.

The fruits of Occupation were smuggled openly.
Customs could not refuse after a honeydew of sorrow.

One epithet is taped inside each suicide silhouette:
"Self-portraits were all the dead drew of sorrow."

I submit this evidence of the masochist's claim—
a sudden hard-on at the slightest blue of sorrow.

With vows of pious smiles mildly veiling their pain,
O how the widowed make a virtue of sorrow!

Of all the stoned prophets, you were the avant-garde:
the chutzpah to declare there's nothing to undo of sorrow!

The god of water's grief ripples through Creation.
Even here in Paradise, the eyes dew of sorrow.

What you do to Time is your business, not mine.
But who is ever late for the curfew of sorrow?

Fuck you, Beautiful! My heart's in jeopardy!
Now tell me which question's untrue of sorrow!

O Blessed Buddha, bitter-less and without pity,
love became exactly what Daniel knew of sorrow.

AT RISK

1.
Cuddling

(You) would not let me
finish the last dirty dish
greased from last night's
mole; instead, (you)—
naked,
seraphim-skinned,
tugging me away
in retreat from morning—
beckoned me back
beneath the bedcovers

There (you),
like warm milk, slid
inside my bends:
fitting so well, I
could have,
like loss,
mistaken myself
for complete

2.
Barebacking

You
medium of my desire
you alone
at this moment
unresisted
are my assassin
if
I mistook
you
for protection.

3.
Remembering

...you,
I will mistake
for everything
worth dying for.

GOSPEL OF MARK

And then you stayed, requiring
a new metaphor to detail the danger:

Glorious as a halo, how you make
men prey in a noose of light.

COMMITMENT

1. How does one forget?
    (a) I'll never close
        my eyes again.
    (b) We shouldn't have fucked so soon.
    (c) *Finding what must suffice,*
        while knowing nothing can suffice.
    (d) *Indeed,*
        I could have loved you better in the dark.

2. Phone call?
    (a) If I could hold
        your memory
        against you,
        then maybe I too
        might forget
        the chronic way
        I wait
        against
        my will.
    (b) *I am come home.*
    (c) All the lines are dead.
    (d) I am now the last
        in the world
        to speak this language.

3. Do you remember each kiss?
   (a) Their names are dismissed tattoos.
   (b) Yes, the ones taken back.
   (c) Only the first and the last.
   (d) Only the next.

4. How will I know it's you?
   (a) It
       will taste
       like
       Yes.
   (b) 姓. . . ?
   (c) *Your laughter pelts my skin with small delicious*
       blows.
   (d) You will have found me yourself.

5. Where do we meet?
   (a) Where it is
                too late, or never—
                the short-time motel.
   (b) *From his*
       Sweet flaming breath
       That proposed an annihilation
       Too real,

       Too
       Beautiful.
   (c) The flash of monsoon
       will make the pavement steam

and smell of jasmine rice
and brown, labored skin.
(d) *You swallowed everything, like distance.*

6. What did you learn of passion?
    (a) He seemed to dance alone.
    (b) The difference if I were a woman.
    (c) It must rain.
    (d) Sexbomb!

7. What can you not see?
    (a) *Every time I backslide, I examine the walls for the traces of my*
        earlier captivities, that is, of my earlier despairs, regrets, and
        desires that some other convict has carved out for me.
    (b) Intention.
    (c) "He looks really hot."
    (d) ...as though
        you didn't
        live
        the life
        you lived.

8. Good?
    (a) Mother Theresa's douche-y
        compared to him.
    (b) so femme
        of you
        to have those eyes

(c) (sigh)

(d) Love the sin.

9. How much is the fare to nowhere?

    (a) I have

                ru ine d

                      my s horeagains tthese frag m e nt   s.

    (b) Be pickin' up bottles'n'cans.

    (c) Is it fare in Nowhere?

    (d) Absolut®

10. What did you say when he asked your name?

    (a) "Could you repeat the question?"

    (b) I wanted to die.

    (c) "I am dying."

    (d) Was I dead?

11. How did you sleep last night?

    (a) Like prose.

    (b) You conquered my thighs.

    (c) The taste of night without

    (d) your arms deliciously
        dressed around
        my sides like a birthday
        cake is a declaration
        of war against the stars

        On these slain

nights I become
an archer and shaman
hunting the musk
and tales of slumber
to mash into a poultice
for our stricken
bodies

Somewhere I
will find the saber
that slashes the cables
of your nightmares
(e) *I kept lament to myself, hid this worry,*
    and let other hands lift you into the grave.

12. Do you know the meaning of my name?
    (a) Plum Illustrious Strong
    (b) I contrive to...
    (c) Does it matter
        if I know
        your tongue?
    (d) It starts with a hush.

13. How many did you count?
    (a) Gone.
    (b) Gone.
    (c) Gone.
    (d) Gone.

14. What is on your plate for tomorrow?

    (a) War is sweet.

    (b) The willed step of our rawness, the unappreciated act of survival.

    (c) Come away with me.

    (d)   *Maybe in this season, drunk*
        and sentimental, I'm willing to admit
        a part of me, crazed and kamikaze,
        ripe for anarchy, loves still.

CARLOS

My mouth

is bittersweeter   with your name

in it

THE NIGHT

String the cellos needed to compose the night
with lines of the sapphire prose: the night.

Eastern stars hasten into a Braille libretto.
Here, caress the encore to close the night.

Oh flame-haired Dutchman, are you now deaf
to the swirl of impasto which flows the night?

Spring's the best *masala* to season the eyes.
Only by hand—grind the rose, the night.

The Tao instructed *yin*, who sought a brother,
"Peel your most passive of foes—the night."

Twilight corroborates a G.I.'s alibi;
For causalities past curfew, he owes the night.

But for heirs sequined with noon bullets,
wail beyond mourning! Impose the night!

If Chaos bore Creation, let us be razed—
cut down by the slayer who knows the night.

Will there be no one to rescue our legends?
Read—one last time—how Daniel froze the night.

FURNISH

What are you doing here, boy,
when there are men out there
whose pockets are train rides
to Tripoli, antique carpets
in the *suuqs* of Marrakech?

You are, like clockwork,
fading hours beneath my hands
keeping me and my poverties company.

So why not have any of those
architects of sonnets
or prodigies of song
willing to exonerate you
from death?

I, artless with verse,
affording little
in the visible world,
have only this—

if you have nothing:
no house
no shadow
and I no house and only a shadow,
should I give you my shadow

make it your home.

BEGINNINGS

Let me be the one who—

Twenty fingers and a few—

Hong Kong, a distance still too—

Ginger-spiked wind blew—

From the waist, slumber grew—

Lines in sand never drew—

Pain too precise to rue—

A half-glass or sudden slew—

The standard lie saw it through—

By SMS, an angel withdrew—

Hesitation frames the true—

Final threat overdue—

Everyday exiles to—

Overcome the need for blue—

You, alas, the last that knew—

What do I do with you—

PROXIMITY

as in nearby:

a boy's hand
shivering with longing
carves the air
just above
his slumbering crush
into a sarcophagus

he can never again
come that close
that vulnerable
to a man

as in almost:

knees flirt
conjoined
a slice of thigh
then calves
get acquainted

mine are in their 30s
shivering
uncertain of whose
turn is it

or if anyone had
made a move

DEATH OF *SAUDADE*

One by one the watches expired
as though they had not been
stamping the cadence of time
but erasing the seconds to

at last

MAKING DINNER

[for Mark Bradbury]

Fingers untucked.
Mint leaves rolled
into a stubby cigar.
Your blade pensively
sliced a chiffonade
sprinkled over
the night's tagine
and a smile weeks later.

"It will take practice,"
one or both of us said,
wondered:

the cutting
or
the craving?

APOCRYPHAL

Before the salt comes
and melts another season
let's just lay down
on this serenade of snow:
you where only letters reach
and I a place with no post office.

If this were a rehearsal for
being together, perhaps
the impressions of our bodies
would appear less like
smudges on winter's cheek
and closer to a footprint—evidence
of a doe—suggesting beyond
speculation, that we
at least
were

THE RAIN

What did you think? That Eternity overcame the rain?
Thus defeated, Lover with Beloved conspired to frame the rain.

The preamble concluded and madness, like Eden, bloomed.
For love's abrupt biography, the heart too took aim: the rain.

Of Earth's disgraced empires who waged the same error—
Romans, Mongols, Ottomans tried fatally to claim the rain.

Which clans are pardoned? Who, with grace, remains?
Surely not parties of grief who contrive to blame the rain.

Not bureaucrats of heaven, nor files of mortal prayers;
The oracle whispers: *Even the Divine wavers to tame the rain.*

Press an ear against his pillow and heed the dark refrain:
Only joy that reaps pain can—at once—maim the rain.

He tries to dull the diamond blade, tries to slow the slaughter—
He who tries to halt a holocaust, tries to rename the rain.

Please do not take photographs only to forget my name.
How did I perish in Memory's attic—the flame? the rain?

I finally wrote that poem for you Daniel. How does it begin?
"Death was a mere formality for your bones became the rain."

Notes on the Text

p. 45 "Commitment"

1c. & 2b. from *The Anxiety of Influence* by Harold Bloom

1d. & 4c. from "Rendezvous" by Edna St. Vincent Millay

5b. from "Too Beautiful" by Hafiz

5d. from "The Song of Despair" by Pablo Neruda

7a. from *Our Lady of the Flowers* by Jean Genet

11d. from "Mourning Lu Yin" by Meng Chiao

14d. from "One Last Poem for Richard" by Sandra Cisneros

p. 64 "Death to *Saudade*"

In Portuguese, *saudade* encompassing nostalgia, longing, melancholy, fondness, hope, love, and missing one who has left without ever knowing if he will ever return. It is said one must *matar as saudades*, or 'kill the saudades' to try to overcome it.